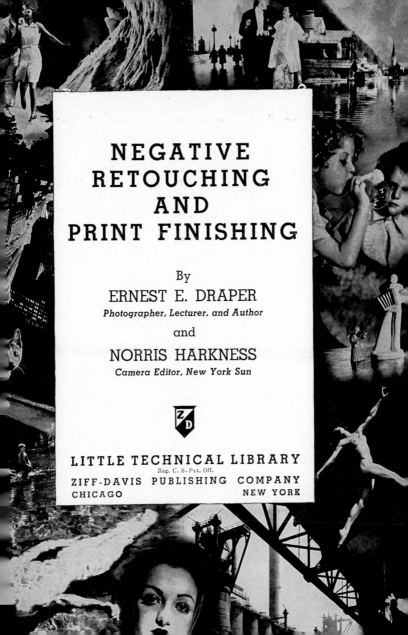

# NEGATIVE RETOUCHING AND PRINT FINISHING

By
### ERNEST E. DRAPER
*Photographer, Lecturer, and Author*

and

### NORRIS HARKNESS
*Camera Editor, New York Sun*

LITTLE TECHNICAL LIBRARY
Reg. U. S. Pat. Off.

ZIFF-DAVIS PUBLISHING COMPANY
CHICAGO                    NEW YORK

ZIFF-DAVIS PUBLISHING COMPANY
CHICAGO          NEW YORK
PRINTED IN THE U.S.A.

## CONTENTS

# CHAPTER 1

## INTRODUCTION

A PICTURE is worth a thousand words—but only if it expresses exactly what we mean without any element that will either distort our intention or reduce its effectiveness. In no other medium can we express what we have to say as clearly as in the photograph, and we have in our camera a tool of unlimited capabilities for such direct expression.

However, it is not often that we can find a subject for our picture that is perfect in every detail. The main theme may express our thought exactly, but its setting may be to some degree detrimental to the perfect understanding on the part of those who will see the picture. Some fundamental element in the principal subject material may need further emphasis, another element must be subdued. We can make our picture tell its final story exactly as we wish it only by the exercise of suitable control in some step of the photographic process.

We may accomplish much of this by selecting the proper viewpoint from which to make the picture when our subject is not under our control, or we can arrange our model and supporting parts of the picture when that is possible. But even when all the factors that control the final effect can be varied to fit our idea, there are still small areas in the picture that do not look in our print just as we saw them in front of the lens.

It is necessary, then, that we have some means by which we can alter relative values in various parts of the picture and, in the case of natural subjects, it is often advantageous to be able to eliminate some parts entirely or bring them into prominence by proper manipulation of the negative or the print, or both. Control in printing by holding back the light from certain portions while others are printed darker, can accomplish this if the area whose tone is to be changed is large. But if that area is relatively small, clumsy dodging or printing-in will betray themselves, and we must resort to some form of retouching in the negative for these finer alterations.

This, of course, removes our picture from the straight record shot class; but ours is an amateur hobby, an activity which we follow because we enjoy it and without thought of pecuniary gain. There is, then, no valid reason for refusing to change the effect of a picture by altering anything in it that will improve the result. No one can question our integrity when we seek to improve our pictures in any way within our command. The picture is what we are after, and the methods by which we obtain that picture cannot be challenged, provided that we do not attempt to pass off the work of another as our own. Our aim is not to reproduce the appearance of a particular place or thing, but to express to the best of our ability the emotion or the mood that made the subject matter attractive to us in the first place.

The negative, with its careful exposure and development, is only the first step in the process of making a picture. Control of atmospheric quality, the attainment of a pleasing and effective composition,* the placing of proper emphasis on the various elements, are all not only possible but, in most cases, can be carried out most efficiently and effectively between the completion of the development of the negative and its insertion into the enlarger for the making of the print.

But resorting to negative manipulation does not mean that we must become a so-called "pictorial photographer." The same technique that the pictorialist utilizes so well will greatly improve many non-pictorial pictures, if we may call them such. Perhaps the test of whether we should adopt some means of control in the negative lies in the answer to the question "how many pictures would you make if you were stranded forever alone on a desert island?" Pictures are made to be seen, and anything that

*This subject is discussed fully in *Composition For The Amateur* (Little Technical Library, No. 4.)

will make them more pleasant and attractive is both legitimate and worthwhile.

Our enjoyment of photography may be derived from large collections of splendid negatives; we may get our fun from building gadgets or from experimenting with photographic chemistry; we may practise any one part of the photographic process with full justification, provided we are getting fun out of using our hobby in that way. The opinion of others as to how we enjoy our hobby has nothing whatever to do with it.

The purpose of this book is to show the ways of improving a picture outside the realms of developing and enlarging which are adequately covered in other volumes of this series. Not only shall we point out many of the things that can be done, but we shall discuss the simplest and easiest ways to accomplish each of them from the whole or partial reduction or intensification of the negative to the toning, spotting, and mounting of the finished print. In other words, it is our plan to present in detail the means by which one can exercise some of the control over subject matter that the artist with his brush or pencil has at his disposal. If he prefers the house or tree here rather than there, and so places them on his canvas, no one complains if the change makes the composition stronger. We have every reason and right to add to the value of our pictures in the same ways, but we must be expert in what we do. There is no crime in improving a picture by anything we can do, provided that we do it so well that no one can see where the work has been done, or find evidence of poor technique or lack of skill.

Many of the processes discussed require practice and the development of a flawless workmanship. None of them, however, is beyond the reach of any amateur who values his picture highly enough to be willing to make some sacrifice to its perfection. We are making pictures for our own pleasure and satisfaction. Let us be satisfied that nothing short of the very best that it is within our power to accomplish.

# CHAPTER II

## THE NEGATIVE

SOMETIMES a negative will not yield a good print because of an error in exposure or development. Before we can attempt any reduction or intensification to compensate for such a mistake, we must be able to recognize the cause of the trouble and judge from the appearance of the negative what the cure will be, and whether it needs much or little correction.

A normally exposed and developed negative—one which we call a normal negative—is one that shows detail in both highlight and shadow areas. It is translucent everywhere, yet has a real deposit of silver even in its thinnest parts, and shows a full range of tones from the darkest gray to the lightest shadow area. The negative with which we are most concerned is intended for enlarging, and is thinner in its over-all density than would be preferred for contact printing, although the difference between the two negatives would be slight.

Negatives vary from the normal in two ways—in density and contrast. **Density,** the strength of the silver deposit throughout the emulsion, depends primarily upon the exposure, and an overexposed negative is very dense with the possibility that the highlights are actually opaque, while the underexposed negative is very thin and, if the underexposure is extreme, will be lacking in shadow detail.

**Contrast,** on the other hand is the result of development. A negative which has been developed for less than the normal time or in a solution whose temperature was too low will be **flat** or **soft,** which simply means that the difference between the highlight and shadow densities is less than it should be. On the other hand, if the development has been carried too far because of errors in timing or temperature, the difference between these two densities will be too great, and the negative will be **contrasty** or **hard.**

Within the ordinary limits of error in either exposure or development, the causes of variation in density or contrast are as stated above. However, if the exposure was much more than it should have been, the negative, even though normally developed, will be lacking in contrast though it is very dense; and a materially underexposed negative will be rather more contrasty than the normal.

The differences, then, by which we can recognize incorrect exposure and development are as follows: The overexposed and overdeveloped negative is dense and slightly contrasty; overexposed and normally developed, it is very dense and slightly flat; overexposed and underdeveloped, it is of normal density and extremely soft. With the so-called "correct" exposure, the overdeveloped negative is slightly dense and quite contrasty; with normal development it is the perfect normal negative, and with underdevelopment it is a little thin and flat. When underexposure has occurred, the overdeveloped negative is probably of about normal density but extremely contrasty; the one normally developed is thin, weak in shadow detail, and slightly flat; and underdeveloped it is too thin to print well, and decidedly lacking in shadow detail.

Blocking up of the highlights (a close approach to opacity in the highlight) is the usual result of too much exposure, while loss of shadow detail is the immediate evidence of an underexposed negative.

With all this in mind we can take up the question of intensification and reduction. As the names of the processes imply, a negative that is too thin to print well will be intensified, and the heavy one will be reduced. However, both of these processes may be carried out so as to increase or decrease the contrast of the negative. We must be sure of the degree of contrast—that is, whether it is already contrasty or soft—before we choose the method that is preferred.

Let us begin with the consideration of the methods of reduction. If the contrast in the dense negative is insufficient and the prints from it are soft, the negative should be reduced in a way that will at once increase the contrast and cut down the over-all density.

There are three types of reducers available for the particular needs of the photographer:

1. The **cutting** or **subtractive** reducer, which increases contrast.
2. The **proportional** reducer, which reduces density evenly in both highlights and shadows.
3. The **superproportional** or **flattening** reducer, which lowers contast as it reduces.

The most commonly used cutting reducer, known as Farmer's Reducer, is a combination of hypo and potassium ferricyanide that acts evenly all over the emulsion and

Fig. I. The upper lefthand corner of this overexposed negative was reduced in a cutting reducer.

Fig. 2. This print was made from the negative shown in Fig. 1.
Notice the improved print quality in portion which was reduced.

therefore has a greater effect on the transparency of the thin parts of the negative. The result is a reduction in density everywhere and an increase in contrast. The Persulfate Reducer is of the flattening type that acts first on the more dense silver deposits and thus, reduces the density and the contrast at the same time. Both of these reducers are progressive, that is, their operation may be stopped whenever the reduction appears to be sufficient. The proportional reducer, a modified two-solution form of Farmer's or a potassium permanganate—ammonium persulfate formula, affects highlights and shadows evenly in the overdeveloped negative.

If a negative is to be reduced in Farmer's Reducer, the operation may be performed immediately after it is taken from the hypo, but if any other reducer is used the negative must be thoroughly washed before reduction is attempted. The negative should be soaked thoroughly in cold water for at least ten minutes before it is placed in

Fig. 3. A negative in which the distant sky area and its reflection are too dense in comparison with the foreground and opposite shore.

Fig. 4. A print made from the negative in Fig. 3 is not satisfactory throughout when exposed properly for the foreground.

the reducing solution, and reduction should be done in short stages, leaving it in the reducer but a short time and transferring it to the rinse for inspection. If it has not been reduced sufficiently, return it to the reducing solution. It is imperative that the negative be removed from the solution and well rinsed in running water before the reduction seems complete; as the chemical reactions continue, they become much more rapid and there is danger of having the reduction go too far. After the process is complete the negative should be thoroughly washed, wiped and dried. This procedure applies to any one-solution reducer, and the directions as given with the formula used should be carried out carefully.

Fig. 1 shows a negative which was materially over-exposed and therefore so dense and flat that it gave a very poor print with a long exposure time. The upper left-hand corner was reduced in Farmer's Reducer. The print, Fig. 2, shows the effect of the reduction in the better

Fig. 5. Dense portions of the negative shown in Fig. 3 were reduced as described in the text, giving it this appearance after treatment.

Fig. 6. Print made from negative on opposite page. Note how local reduction brings out detail in distant peaks (see Fig. 4).

tones, increased depth and roundness, and generally better print quality.

Sometimes we desire to reduce only some small section of the negative to correct the balance in the tones of the various areas. When this is desired the negative should be soaked as before, on a horizontal glass, and patted dry with a viscose sponge or a chamois. The reducer is then applied to the desired parts with a bit of cotton or a camel hair brush. If the brush is used, care must be taken that no iron or other metal touch the reducer, or blue spots on the negative will result.

Here again the action must not be allowed to go too far, and it is much better to permit the chemicals to work for perhaps half a minute and then rinse the negative, sponge it again, and apply more of the reducer. This can be repeated as many times as may seem necessary, but care must be taken to blend the reduced area into the remainder of the negative so that no hard line will show in the print. Of course, a negative so treated needs thorough washing after the operation is finished.

Fig. 3 shows the negative from which Fig. 4 was made. The sky area and its reflection in the water are so dense in comparison to the shadow areas in the foreground that a satisfactory print could not be made; detail in the mountains is almost lost, while there is no tone in the sky. Even on soft paper a satisfying print is impossible. However, Farmer's Reducer was applied with cotton to the negative, Fig. 5. The result was that when Fig. 6 was printed on normal paper, the sky had a tone and a suggestion of clouds, while the mountains are perfectly distinct. And here a word of caution. These processes are corrective and alter tonal relationships and values in the picture. We must be careful, therefore, to use them judiciously in order to avoid the creation of an unnatural and synthetic atmosphere that, while the observer may not be able to identify the cause of the trouble, will nevertheless prevent his complete enjoyment of the picture. Negatives to be reduced should first be hardened in a formalin hardener, using the formula given on page 24.

## Formulas for Reduction

Farmer's Reducer for correcting overexposed negatives is made by taking a 10 per cent solution of hypo and adding enough of a 5 per cent solution of potassium ferricyanide to make it appear lemon yellow in daylight. It must be discarded after use since it keeps only a short time. Mix only what is needed for your negative. The more ferricyanide there is in the solution, the quicker the reducing action. The hypo acts as a check on the ferricyanide.

It is possible to use Farmer's Reducer as a two-solution reducer. This gives proportional reduction to over-developed negatives.

### Two-Solution Farmer's Reducer—Kodak R-4b

| Solution A | Avoirdupois | Metric |
|---|---|---|
| Potassium ferricyanide ................ | ¼ ounce | 7.5 grams |
| Water to make........................ | 32 ounces | 1.0 liter |
| Solution B | | |
| Sodium thiosulfate (Hypo)............... | 6¾ ounces | 200.0 grams |
| Water to make........................ | 32 ounces | 1.0 liter |

The negatives should be treated in Solution A with uniform agitation for 1 to 4 minutes at 65 to 70 degrees F., depending on the extent of reduction desired. They should then be immersed in Solution B for 5 minutes and washed thoroughly.

### Proportional Reducer—Kodak R-5

| Solution A | Avoirdupois | Metric |
|---|---|---|
| Water ............................... | 32 ounces | 1.0 liter |
| Potassium permanganate ................ | 4 grains | 0.3 gram |
| Sulfuric acid (10% solution)........... | ½ fl. ounce | 16.0 cc. |
| | | |
| Solution B | | |
| Water ............................... | 96 ounces | 3.0 liters |
| Ammonium persulfate ................. | 3 ounces | 90.0 grams |

Take one part of A to three parts of B. When sufficient reduction is secured, the negative should be cleared in a one per cent solution of sodium bisulfite. Wash it thoroughly before drying.

### Superproportional Reducer—Kodak R-1

For correcting overdeveloped negatives of contrasty subjects.

| Solution A | Avoirdupois | Metric |
|---|---|---|
| Ammonium persulfate ................. | 2 ounces | 60 grams |
| *Sulfuric acid (pure conc.).............. | ¾ dram | 3 cc. |
| Water to make........................ | 32 ounces | 1 liter |

*Sulfuric acid must be added to the water, otherwise the solution may boil with explosive violence and may cause serious burns on hands or face. Take one part of the above solution and two parts of water. A slight milkiness of the solution indicates start of the reduction. Once started this action is rapid, and must be watched carefully from this point. When the desired reduction has been secured, immerse the negative quickly in an acid fixing bath for a few minutes, and wash thoroughly before drying. The solution can be diluted with an equal volume of water to slow up the reducing action. The negative must be free from hypo before treatment with persulfate.

Intensifiers, too, may be used to increase or decrease contrast while they build up the density of the negative. Where a great amount of intensification is desired a simple method is to treat it as though it were to be sepia toned, bleaching it in the ferricyanide-bromide solution exactly as though it were a print, and darkening the image in sodium sulfide.

The most frequently used intensifiers are the mercury and chromium formulas.

Figs. 7 to 10 show the effect of intensification to increase contrast. The original negative (Fig. 7) is thin and lacking in contrast; it was underexposed and then

Fig. 7, below, shows a thin negative which was underexposed and then underdeveloped. A print from this negative is flat and uninteresting, as shown in Fig. 8, opposite.

underdeveloped. The best print is flat and uninteresting, as shown in Fig. 8. After the negative was intensified by the chromium treatment it appeared as shown in Fig. 9, and yielded the print in Fig. 10. Notice here, however, an important point. Despite the intensification, there is no more shadow detail in Fig. 10 than there was in Fig. 8, and no intensification can supply details whose lack is due to underexposure. If those details are not in the negative because of sufficient exposure, we cannot put them in by any chemical means. So, while intensification and reduction may help a picture greatly they can only correct partially for our previous errors.

Fig. 9. The negative (Fig. 7) was intensified by the chromium method, and is greatly
improved. It now produces a much better
print, shown in Fig. 10 on page opposite.

## Formulas for Intensification

A good chromium intensifier formula is as follows:

### Chromium Intensifier—Kodak In-4

| Stock Solution | Avoirdupois | Metric |
|---|---|---|
| Potassium bichromate | 3 ounces | 90.0 grams |
| Hydrochloric acid (conc.) | 2 fl. ounces | 64.0 cc. |
| Water to make | 32 ounces | 1.0 liter |

Take 1 part of stock solution and 10 parts of water. Harden the negative first in a formalin hardener (see below). Bleach thoroughly in the bichromate solution at 65 to 70 degrees F. After washing for five minutes, redevelop (in artificial light or daylight, but not direct sunlight) in any Elon-hydroquinone developer which does not contain an excess of sulfite. It will take from 3 to 10 minutes, depending on the amount of intensification desired. Then rinse the negative, place it in a fixing bath for about 5 minutes, then wash thoroughly. If more intensification is wanted, repeat the process.

The formalin hardener is important because most intensifiers soften the gelatin, and should be used with all formulas.

### Formalin Hardener—Kodak SH-1

| | Avoirdupois | Metric |
|---|---|---|
| Formalin (37% formaldehyde solution) | 2½ drams | 10.0 cc. |
| Sodium carbonate (desiccated) | 73 grains | 5.0 grams |
| Water to make | 32 ounces | 1.0 liter |

After treatment in this solution for 3 minutes, wash for 10 minutes, then immerse in a 2 per cent solution of acetic acid and rinse. Handle only one negative at a time, and agitate during the entire treatment . Intensify before drying.

A one-solution formula in which the progress of intensification can be watched and stopped at any point is the mercuric iodide intensifier:

| | Avoirdupois | Metric |
|---|---|---|
| Mercuric iodide | ⅔ ounce | 20.0 grams |
| Potassium iodide | ⅔ ounce | 20.0 grams |
| Hypo (crystals) | ⅔ ounce | 20.0 grams |
| Water to make | 32 ounces | 1.0 liter |

Dissolve the chemicals in an ounce of warm water before diluting to volume. This solution can be used repeatedly until it is exhausted. If the result is unsatisfactory, the intensification can be removed or reduced in a 20 per cent hypo solution. This must be done before any further after-treatment is attempted. The image is not permanent, but can be made satisfactorily so by immersing the negative in any Elon-hydroquinone developer or a 1 per cent solution of sodium sulfide, such as is used regularly for sulfide toning.

Some of the chemicals used in reducers and intensifiers are poisonous and should be handled carefully. It is also wise to experiment with the solution you plan to use before entrusting a valued negative to it.

A method of cutting down the density in small areas in the negative is the use of alcohol and elbow grease. A small wad of cotton saturated with the alcohol and then squeezed almost dry is rubbed over the area to be reduced until it removes enough silver to reduce the density. If the area is large, the wad may be held in the fingers, but for small patches it would be better to twist the cotton around the pointed end of a match stick. The rubbing should be very gentle at first; soon a black deposit will appear on the cotton, after which the action will be much faster. This method of reduction offers a disadvantage if the negative is to be retouched later, since it leaves the emulsion with a shiny surface that will not take pencil easily. Of course, a negative so treated does not need to be washed, though it will probably be a good idea to swab off the entire surface with clean alcohol when the reduction is completed.

But all this presupposes the use of fairly large negatives, and local control of miniature negatives is very nearly impossible. However, users of small cameras will find that they can obtain the same results by making a larger positive, doing the necessary control operations on it, and then making another negative that will fit their enlargers. Any size positive can be used, of course, but 5x7 is very convenient and not too expensive.

The procedure is as follows: Place a piece of white paper in the correct size printing frame, place the negative you wish to control in the enlarger, and focus it in the required size on that paper. Then replace the paper with a Commercial film or plate (the glass plate is easier to handle than cut film) and make the necessary exposure. Since the plate is much faster than any enlarging paper, it will be necessary to reduce the light intensity in the enlarger by stopping down the lens as much as possible and interposing either a few layers of tissue paper above the condenser or diffuser, or a light yellow filter over the lens. The exposure should be full so that a comparatively short development will give a positive that is full-bodied and not too contrasty. The result will be better if the plate lies on black paper during the exposure to prevent the softening effect of reflections from the back of the glass while the light is on. Use a safelight suitable to the film in place of the one used for paper.

The modifications can be carried out on this positive if we remember that we are now working with a positive, or we can make a contact negative from the positive on another similar film or plate. This exposure, of course, will be extremely short, and a 10-watt bulb some 8 feet away will give sufficient light. Again the exposure should be fairly full, and the development kept to the minimum. This will give a negative that can be enlarged as much as desired after further manipulation, if such is required. If, however, the enlarger will not accommodate the bigger film or plate, the desired changes can be made on the positive, and a new negative made by photographing the positive while it is illuminated uniformly from behind.

Another entirely photographic. means of decreasing contrast is to make a contact print on a small glass plate. A short exposure and short development will give only the shadow areas a chance to show on the plate. When dry, this positive image is fastened in perfect register to the negative with Scotch tape, and the final print is made through the combination.

A practical method of holding back shadows is the application of **neococcin** to the thin areas of the negative. This is a red analine dye that comes in powder form. A very small amount of the powder is dissolved in a considerable quantity of water—very little color should be used at one time—and it is applied to the negative with a camel hair brush or cotton. The brush should be almost dry in putting the color on the emulsion to avoid wetting it so much that it swells or forms blisters, and repeated applications are far better than trying to deposit sufficient tone in one operation. In applying neococcin the real secret of success is to use as little color as possible on the brush, and then blot the area immediately after the application to keep it from affecting the gelatin too much. Use a good quality, hard-surface photographic blotter that does not leave lint on the film.

In some cases the emulsion may have been so hardened that it may refuse to absorb the color. If this occurs, a very weak solution of ammonia may be applied to the area we desire to color, but only a slight amount of ammonia should be used; if too much of the alkali is applied the color may cause the gelatin to break down, and it will be then impossible to keep the trouble from showing on the print. Sometimes a little saliva rubbed over the areas will serve as well as the diluted ammonia.

Neococcin actually has more effect on the print than one suspects when applying it to the negative. This means, then, that until we are thoroughly familiar with its use, we must make repeated trials in order to get enough color into the film without making those areas print too light. If, on trial, we find that we have used too much color, we can eliminate it by soaking the entire negative in a very weak solution of ammonia, or by laying a bit of cotton saturated with the ammonia solution over the colored areas and then washing the film thoroughly.

A method that probably gives us the greatest possible control over the tones in our picture might be called pigment control. There are many ways of using it that differ principally in the materials used and in the size in which we wish to work. The most perfect system is to make an enlarged positive on which any of the control processes can be practiced, and then make a negative the same size as our final prints. The same plan is entirely applicable to smaller negatives which will later be enlarged.

The method consists of attaching the negative to glass and coating that glass with groundglass substitute, or covering the negative with finegrain tracing paper, Traceoline, or similar material. If the groundglass substitute method is to be followed, the glass is flowed evenly with the liquid and the negative is fastened to the clear side of the glass with Scotch tape, with its emulsion toward the glass. This is a permanent fastening which will remain throughout the printing. If Traceoline or tracing paper is used, the material may be taped directly to the emulsion side of the negative.

We shall work by transmitted light (see Chapter III for the details of a simple retouching stand), and shall apply the pigment to the groundglass or the Traceoline.

There are many pigments which can be used. Very small areas will best be covered with a sharply pointed, medium-soft pencil along the general lines outlined for retouching in Chapter III. Larger areas can be darkened most easily by rubbing powder black, graphite, charcoal, crayon sauce, or even stove blacking into the working surface. One of the most convenient materials is the graphite which can be obtained in block form from any artists' supply store—the very soft grade (6B) is best.

A piece of blotter or the cover of a small cardboard box makes an excellent pallet. A small amount of the pigment is placed on the pallet (a vigorous rubbing of the crayon or graphite will supply enough) and applied with a wad of cotton on large areas, or with a smaller bit of cotton on the end of a pointed match stick to smaller sections.

Working in a darkened room by transmitted light will enable you to determine accurately whether enough tone has been applied to the area as you go along, and when the job is almost complete a test print will show exactly where further treatment may be needed. If too much pigment is applied in some part of the picture, it can be removed with an art gum or kneaded eraser. The kneaded eraser is especially valuable because it does not leave crumbs on the surface, and can be moulded in the fingers to the size and shape of the working point that will be most convenient.

We said above that working in the full size of the final picture is best. This is because we can judge more easily the exact effect of the changes made, and also because alterations can be made on both the positive and the negative. On the enlarged positive (called the "dia-positive") we can use the pigment to darken objectionable highlights, the corners of the print, or any other areas that we wish to have darker in the print. In the same way we can add pigment to those parts of the negative that we wish to make lighter in the final picture, and every small section is completely under our control. The two

Fig. 11. A straight print made from the entire negative of a farmyard scene.

full-size transparencies are fairly expensive, but the results obtainable and the ease and accuracy with which one can work make this method so superior that it should not be ignored.

Fig. 11 shows the print from the whole negative of a farmyard scene. Taken as a whole, it leaves much to be

Fig. 12. Enlarged film diapositive and retouched groundglass.

desired as a picture, and extraneous material must be eliminated while the important elements need emphasis and relief. Then too, the more distant fence posts are not attractive and they can be eliminated. A diapositive the size of the final print, and including only the material desired in that print, was made by straight enlargement. This was attached to a sheet of glass covered with ground-glass substitute as just described. Both of these are shown in Fig. 12, and in this illustration we can see how various areas in the print were darkened and changed to make the picture more nearly in accordance with our plans (Fig. 13). Additional changes could have been made had it been found desirable, but this amount of retouching

Fig. 13. Negative made from combined diapositive and groundglass was used to make this print.

seemed to be adequate and so the picture was left this way

The methods discussed above are adapted principally to the alteration and control of tone values in the whole negative or in small areas, though some of them may be used to eliminate completely undesirable elements from the picture. There are times, however, when we cannot avoid a confusing background in making the shot, and in such cases we can resort to removing this undesired background, making it print either perfectly white or entirely black. To block out a background we can paint the negative with a reddish-brown material known as **Opaque**. The light cannot penetrate the Opaque and the print is, therefore, white in these areas. The main difficulty with this system is the fact that the edge of the opaqued area is likely to be hard and unpleasant. Softening this edge may be accomplished with the aid of retouching medium and penciling, or by applying a heavy border of neococcin as outlined in Chapter III. The commercial photographer who knows when he makes a picture that the background will be opaqued in this way, outlines his subject sharply by photographing it against a contrasting background color. A dark object, for example, would be shown against a light background, and vice versa. Since the background will not show, he can use cloth or paper against which to silhouette the important parts. When this has been done, it is a simple matter to outline the picture with a brush or with a ruling pen, filling in the remaining area afterward. This results in a picture silhouetted against a white background.

Should a black background be preferred, the emulsion may be removed from around the principal objects. A sharp etching knife is used to scrape off all the emulsion except the objects of interest which are to be retained and which will then print against a black background. Here again the main difficulty is at the edge of the actual picture, and the etching should begin at the outlines that are to be kept while one works away from those areas. Dampening the emulsion that is to be removed will sim-

Fig. 14. Straight print from negative. The cow was photographed against a dull sky.

Fig. 15. White background
obtained by blocking negative.

Fig. 16. Etched negative produces black background on print

plify the work. The etching task is not one which should
be undertaken carelessly, and considerable practice is
necessary before a satisfactory job can be made of it.

Fig. 14 is a straight print from the whole negative of
"Pansy," who was photographed against a dull sky. As a
preface to the substitution of a new background for her,
the original background was blocked out (Fig. 15), and
later etched out (Fig. 16). Neither process is especially
conducive to pictorialism, but they do permit the amateur
to remove unpleasant things in preparation for the inclus-
ion of better settings for the main objects in the picture.

A satisfying way to substitute a more suitable background for one which is less pleasant is illustrated
in Figs. 17, 18, 19. The shot of the child was made against
dark bushes through which the light showed in irregular
blotches, and the background was too dark to be appropriate to the life in the child's face. To paint in or otherwise construct a fitting background was very difficult, so
a cloud print was made in addition to the print of the
child, both on singleweight paper. With the child's head
in the right spot on the cloud print, which could be established by viewing them both by transmitted light, and held
firmly in place with rubber cement, a sharp knife was run

34

Fig. 17. Snapshot of child taken in back yard against a background of dark bushes.

Fig. 18. Figure of child was cut out of the print and combined with enlarged cloud print.

Fig. 19. The pasteup shown in Fig. 18 was photographed, and a print from the copy negative matted to produce this attractive portrait study.

around the outline of the child's picture, cutting through both prints to make the two parts fit together exactly. The two parts of the final print were cemented down in jigsaw fashion on a card. Rough work with a pencil hid the marks and faults of the cutting, and the pasteup was photographed to make the picture shown in Fig. 19.

You have seen that many of the mistakes in the exposure or development of the negative can be corrected, and that the quality of a print can be improved tremendously by bettering the relationships of tonal values in large or small areas. The negative is only the means to an end, and we must do all in our power to make it as near perfect as possible through any medium at our command.

## CHAPTER III

### NEGATIVE RETOUCHING

IN no branch of photography is the ability to make changes in the negative as important as it is in portraiture. In the first place, every portrait subject has facial faults that add nothing to the beauty of the picture, and these imperfections are emphasized by the lighting which the photographer must use to separate the planes of the face and give the picture depth and roundness. Sidelighting throws deep shadows into the lines of the face, and makes them seem sharper and deeper in the photograph than they do when we look at the subject. Moreover, every person likes to be portrayed as he would prefer to look rather than as nature made him, and the pose that helps us to achieve this result often causes a sudden attack of double chins or wrinkles. Add to all these things the fact that the film records every detail with a color sensitivity that does not agree with our vision, and we have more than enough reason to learn retouching.

Lines and wrinkles become less prominent as soon as we make them print in a lighter tone, and poorly placed highlights and the shine on the curved surface of a double chin can be etched away to give a nicely graded tone. The etching knife can also act as lady's maid in eliminating stray locks of hair and straightening eyebrows, and there are few portraits that can be submitted without any retouching.

This is borne out by the experience of the professional photographer who retouches not only the final picture but also most of the negatives from which he will make proofs. He has found that he cannot sell a portrait unless it has been worked upon enough to bring out the good points of the face and remove the blemishes and faults. In many cases where the subject is sufficiently attractive, the use of a soft-focus lens or diffusion in the printing will hide the things we do not wish to show, but these subterfuges are rapidly becoming recognizable as such by an ever increasing proportion of the general public. So one cannot expect to establish a reputation as a portrait photographer unless he is able to learn at least the simpler types of retouching.

Many photographers prefer to use orthochromatic film because they feel that with it they obtain better flesh tones and roundness; but they know that this red-blind emulsion will print any brown or red tone considerably darker than it appears to the eye. Red lips become black, and small pimples or other skin blemishes show up strongly. This is the kind of film to use in order to bring out freckles on the face of the small boy; but it is definitely not the film to use on the beautiful lady with the auburn hair, unless one is prepared to retouch innumerable fine veins and spots on the face which show on the negative but which are completely invisible as we look at her.

Panchromatic film, on the other hand, prints all these minor blemishes in a lighter tone that practically matches the skin color and, if the subject is properly lighted, leaves little to be desired in roundness and flesh tones. The amateur who does not wish to spend hours over the retouching desk will probably find panchromatic film preferable.

The necessary materials are few and simple. We need a light box or other arrangement by which we can see the negative entirely by transmitted light. The stand shown in Fig. 20 is easy to construct and works in very satisfactory fashion. It consists of two boards 12 inches square, hinged together at one end and spread at the opposite end by removable props which are pivoted to one board to become an integral part of the stand. The upper board—the working surface—is cut out and a piece of ground or opal glass either lies over the hole or is set into it.

Fig. 20. The negative is placed over the illuminated groundglass on the retouching stand.

The inner surface of the lower board should either be painted white or covered with a white card or paper. An ordinary desk light is then placed so that its rays are reflected from the white surface to the glass on which the negative lies while the retouching is done. The work will best be accomplished in a rather dark room so that all the light used comes through the negative and one is not annoyed or mislead by reflections from the surface of the film. It is usually preferable to cover the negative with a piece of black paper in which a hole 2 inches in diameter has been torn. The hole can be moved from place to place as we work on different areas. This system reduces glare and eye strain, and enables us to concentrate better on the area in question. Lacking opal or groundglass we can do satisfactory work with a piece of plain glass set in the upper board and with a diffusion screen of paper or Traceoline placed behind it. These retouching stands may be made in some fashion as shown, or purchased complete from any photographic supply store.

The tools used are an etching knife, a stone to sharpen it (the one known to the trade as the Arkansas stone is preferred), spotting brushes and colors like those used for spotting prints, retouching medium, retouching pencils, cotton, fine emery cloth or sandpaper, neococcin (or a newer product, Spotone, which works in the same way but is practically the same color as the negative), and Opaque. None of these items is expensive, and all of them last for a very long time. If the negatives are to be enlarged, it is advisable to procure a magnifying glass and obtain or make some stand to hold it at the required distance from the negative, in order to examine the work. The pencils for the beginner should be rather hard (3H or 4H), for with a softer pencil he is likely to put on too much lead and obtain a grainy texture in the lighter areas of the print. The more experienced worker will want a number of pencils of varying hardness for different purposes.

The pencils need a very long and exceedingly sharp

point, and it is best to use the fine sandpaper or emery cloth to obtain this kind of point. In sharpening the pencil, hold the elbows tight against the sides, and with the lead in a fold of the abrasive material, move the pencil back and forth and turn it around while maintaining a firm, but not too strong, pressure against the emery cloth. The point should be like that of a needle, and needs to be kept as sharp as possible through repeated resharpenings. Fig. 21 shows the method of sharpening.

The etching knife, too, must be kept razor-sharp, for a dull knife will always result in uneven and scratchy areas on the print. When you purchase it, notice that its ground surface is at an angle of about thirty degrees to the face of the blade, and that this surface is the only one that is ground at all. It is important to maintain this angle carefully if the knife is to serve you properly. Before you begin to sharpen the blade, find the correct angle at

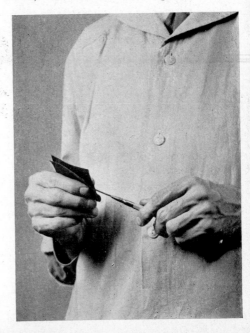

Fig. 21. The long retouching lead is sharpened to a very fine point with a folded piece of sandpaper or emery cloth.

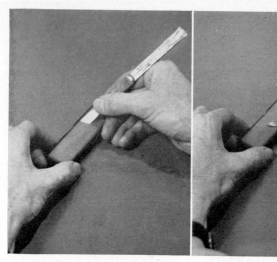

Fig. 22. Correct way to hold etching knife on the whetstone.

Fig. 23. Burr is removed after sharpening in the manner shown.

which to hold it on the stone, as shown above in Fig. 22. The motion used in sharpening is always toward the back of the right hand shown in the illustration, and the blade must never be pushed back and forth with pressure in both directions. Check the appearance of the ground surface frequently to be sure you are not changing the angle, and when the grinding seems complete remove the tiny burr that forms on the face by placing that surface flat on the stone as shown in Fig. 23 and moving it gently with a circular motion until the edge is smooth. The knife is then ready to use.

We have made a test print like that shown in Fig. 24 and have decided which areas need attention and what treatment each one shall be given. The hair, the bulge in the shirt, the catchlight in the right eye, and a few spots and marks need to be etched, so we place the negative (Fig. 25) on the stand and proceed to use the knife. The etching knife has for its sole purpose the removal of a tiny layer of the emulsion. Since the entire emulsion

42

Fig. 24. Test print made from the unretouched portrait negative.

is only a few thousandths of an inch in thickness, it is obvious that etching is a delicate operation, and should be practiced on worthless film until it has been mastered. The knife is held so that the plane of the ground surface is at an angle to the emulsion but with the long edge very nearly parallel to it, and the motion is a gentle, scraping sweep. There is never any picking movement of the blade except in those instances where a tiny round spot is to be eliminated, and even then the picking is almost certain to require spotting or retouching with the pencil afterward.

Gently and carefully then, we scrape away the stray hairs and the dark spot on the upper forehead. With the greatest possible care the catchlight in the right eye is reduced until it matches the left one. The bulge in the shirt is smoothed out by removing its dark edge in the negative. When these areas suit us—and it will pay to be very particular and fussy—we are ready for the reduction of the prominent highlight on the wrist. This area is too big to be etched, so we resort to the alcohol and cotton abrasive method outlined in Chapter II, and rub down the dark area until the tone is less noticeable.

We have decided that the dark line from the left corner of the mouth to the side of the nose must be lightened in the print, and also that this area is too large to be penciled, so we use neococcin to darken it in the negative. With a faint pink liquid and an almost dry brush we add a very slight tone to the deepest shadow until it seems right. The same material or spotting color is used to fill in the scratch opposite the right eyebrow.

Now we are ready for the penciling. Naturally the shiny emulsion will not take the pencil lead, and must be roughened to give it the needed "tooth." As shown in Fig. 26, a drop or two of the retouching medium is placed in the middle of the negative with the cork of the bottle and then quickly rubbed all over the negative with cotton or soft tissue. The medium need not cover the entire surface, but to avoid any possibility of having it show on the print, it is better to soften the edge of the place it covers by a brisk circular motion of the cotton, followed

Fig. 26. Retouching medium is applied to emulsion side of the negative with cotton.

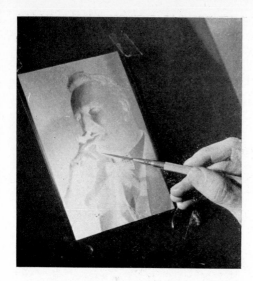

by smaller circles around the edges of the spot. Fairly rapid but gentle rubbing will give a nice distribution of the medium, which dries almost immediately. This medium is rubbed directly on the emulsion in all ordinary cases, but if enough tone cannot be added in some part of the picture we may turn the negative over, rub the medium on the back of the negative, and add more lead to those places on that side as well.

If too much medium has been used it will not dry thoroughly, but will remain in a gummy state that picks up too much lead and collects dust and lint. In such an event the application of more medium and brisk rubbing with dry cotton will probably remove the surplus, or all of it can be removed with cotton dampened with alcohol. With the right amount, the negative is ready for the retouching.

The purpose, of course, is to add lead to the thin areas of the negative until they have a printing density that will give the effect desired, but we cannot simply smear the surface with long strokes of the pencil. Holding the pencil lightly and as shown in Fig. 27, we work over the lines at the corner of the left eye, not to eliminate them com-

Fig. 28. Print from retouched negative. Compare it with Fig. 24.

pletely, but to make them slightly lighter in tone. The spot over that eye needs to be made to match the tones immediately surrounding, and the edges of the neococcin application must be blended suitably. The shirt that was etched before needs to be given a new straight line, and the various small skin blemishes will all need lead. A little experimenting will show the most comfortable and effective angle at which to hold the pencil, but the pressure will always be very light. The point must be resharpened continually to keep it in good working condition. In using the pencil, various retouchers have different techniques. One worker fills in an area with innumerable tiny semicircles or fish hooks; another covers the area with little S's; still others have their own comfortable mark that gradually and almost imperceptibly fills in an area and blends it with the tones around it.

If we are to maintain any strength and character in our portraits we shall not eliminate lines, but only lighten them. Without them the face becomes a mere mask, and with them the picture is unpleasant. However, we can lighten them to the right degree and achieve a print that is at once a good likeness and an attractive picture.

A comparison of Fig. 24 with Fig. 28 show the changes that the retouching has accomplished. But suppose that Fig. 28 had not given the desired results. It would be a simple matter to use more retouching medium or alcohol to remove all the penciling that was done, so that we might begin again. If, however, too much lead had been added in only a few places, we could resort to the etching knife and remove the surplus.

And now for a few general hints on the whole subject of retouching. Get a good etching knife, keep it clean and sharp, and use it only for retouching. Always use it gently to shave the emulsion rather than to pick out small spots. Use as little retouching medium as is needed to cover the negative area, and apply it as smoothly as you can. Don't attempt too much change in a portrait, but consider that retouching is for corrective purposes, rather than for major operations. Be sure that the catchlights n the eyes match as to position and size, and that there is only one in each eye.

If you can find an area that has no silver in it and that s too shiny and smooth to take the lead, roughen it with a gentle scrape of the etching knife and then use the pencil. Above all, remember that retouching is an art that requires great concentration and practice. Remember too, that a retouched negative is likely to collect dust and dirt, and smudges easily; protect it with an envelope.

A properly retouched negative will retain all the realism of one that has not been worked upon, and at the same time it will gain in brilliance, effectiveness of tone, and especially in the elimination of its less attractive elements. Retouching is not something to be approached casually, but it is a worthwhile tool that is as valuable as our willingness to become proficient makes it. No portrait photographer can afford to try to do without it.

# CHAPTER IV

## THE PRINT

IT is not in the province of this book to discuss enlarging methods which have been covered in another volume of this series.* We do, however, want to discuss the things that can be done to the print after it is fixed and washed. Some of these are small and seemingly unimportant details, but if they are omitted or carelessly carried out, the picture will fall short of the success it really merits. We shall not attempt to take these up in the order in which they would be used, because this sequence varies from picture to picture. But we emphasize the importance of proper attention to each of them. If genius is the infinite capacity for taking pains, a perfect picture is the result of coordinated and thorough-going skill and workmanship through every step of the process.

It is difficult to select the viewpoint and frame the photograph so perfectly in the field that the whole negative contains all that is needed without extraneous and distracting details. In the great majority of our prints we have to choose judiciously the exact borders of the final picture. This trimming away of unessential subject matter is known as **cropping,** and it is one of the most important steps through which our picture must go. Too often we are led by the size and shape of the paper at hand to force our picture into just those dimensions instead of letting the arrangement of the subject matter decide the shape of the picture. But this was not intended to be a chapter on composition.

To get back to the subject of cropping and how is it best done, many of our finest pictorialists make a test print of the entire negative on cheap singleweight paper.

*This subject is discussed in *Manual of Enlarging* (Little Technical Library, No. 15.)

Fig. 29. Print showing better placement of subject by cropping. Compare with Fig. 14 on page 33.

From it they decide just what alterations will help the general effect, and exactly what the framing of the picture will be. The framing is greatly facilitated by the use of two cardboard "L's," with each arm two or three inches wide and long enough to cover the greatest dimension likely to be encountered in a print. These are arranged overlapping each other so as to form a rectangular opening through which the picture and its composition can be studied, and either "L" may be moved so as to include more or less of the contents of the print. When we have finally decided on the best limits to which we shall make the final print the edges can be marked on this test print for reference in making the enlargement.

The great gains that we can make by proper cropping are shown by a comparison of Figs. 14 and 29. In the first, which shows the whole negative, the cow's head is badly placed. There is much wasted space that contributes nothing to the picture and is, therefore, definitely detrimental to it. The cropped version in Fig. 29 is far stronger. In the same way extraneous detail has been eliminated from the cluttered scene of Fig. 11 to make the picture in Fig. 30. These pictures were cropped for different reasons, but both have gained immensely in simplicity and unity by cropping. In many cases we shall find that running the two cardboard "L's" over our finest pictures as well as over those that are less successful will at once show us stronger and better compositions by the elimination of unnecessary elements and the consequent concentration of interest on the really important things in the picture.

Now comes the question of toning and the equally important question of when to tone. It generally happens that when we are introduced to a new toning formula every print we make for the next few weeks is put through that solution. This is fun, to do but it is not conducive to the best possible pictures. A snow scene, for example, should never be sepia or brown, and blue toning is almost always unsatisfactory if not actually unpleasant for woodland scenes. We must remember the psychological effect of color, and make sure that the tone that we give the print fits the subject matter and the mood or emotion that caused us to make the shot in the first place. The straight black-and-white photograph may or may not be the most effective picture of an individual scene, but the burden of proof must rest upon the toning rather than upon the black-and-white, and something in the picture must definitely demand representation in a particular color. For example, a man's portrait might well be sepia, while the winter landscape is better in blue provided we have the right shade of blue. A deep woodland scene would require a deeper brown than did the portrait, and a reddish brown might be preferable for a fall landscape.

But the selection of the proper tone cannot be left to such general classifications as these. We said that the blue of a winter scene must be the right blue. In the same way the picture of a young, attractive blonde in high key will be better in sepia with a slightly reddish tinge, and her older brunette sister will look better with a more blue-brown tone. The winter landscape will look coldest with a real blue, while a marine would want a

Fig. 30. Another example showing how careful cropping eliminates unnecessary detail and improves the composition of a picture (see Fig. 11, page 29).

blue more toward the green side. Toning is not a subject that can be learned thoroughly from the printed page, but one can study the fundamentals and gain many helpful ideas. We can only obtain the effect that seems best by experimentation and trial and error.

With our picture properly printed, cropped, and toned the question of spotting comes next. The best time to do the spotting is before you get the spots, and the careful worker keeps his negatives and the negative carrier in the enlarger as clean and as free from dust as is possible. However, it is almost impossible to produce a print that has none of the light spots caused by dust on or near the negative when the exposure was made, and they must be removed from the prints before they can be shown as finished photographs. Scratches or pinholes in the negative cause dark spots on the print, and these, too, must be eliminated. The etching knife can be used for these spots on the print in exactly the method described for etching a negative. With a little practice one can reduce a very dark spot to the tone surrounding it without any further treatment. If, however, we find that we have etched too deeply and made the spot too light, we can darken it with spotting colors and brush.

As shown in Fig. 31, materials needed are spotting colors which are sold on cards (black, white, sepia and other colors) and a good quality camel hair brush that forms a sharp point when moist. Cheap brushes may be used, but they must be carefully selected to get one that "points" up well; the size called No. 0 is most satisfactory.

The secret of successful spotting is moderation. The brush should not carry too much color, nor should it be more than barely moistened. Saliva is an excellent liquid with which to work as the colors stick better to the print than they do when pure water is used. The wet brush is run through the color until it collects a rather large amount which is transferred to the clean edge of the color card, or to a piece of glass or porcelain. This somewhat diluted color becomes the source of supply, and various colors can be mixed together to match the color of the print.

Fig. 31. Spotting color is removed from card with a wet brush.

Fig. 32. Excess color is removed from brush on sheet of paper.

The fairly heavily charged brush is then drawn over a sheet of absorbent paper as shown in Fig. 32, until it leaves only a very faint line, and then we are ready to begin work on the print itself. Check the color in the margin of the print to make sure that the tone or color has been matched correcly, then begin actual spotting in the darker areas of the picture.

The brush is held almost perpendicular to the print as shown in Fig. 33, and is moved in a stippling motion. There is never any occasion for a painter's technique, and the area, regardless of its size, will be filled in with a great many tiny dots (see Fig. 34). If the spot is small, perhaps one or two dots will hide it, but if it is large, we must begin at the edges and work toward the middle, matching the new tone to the old as we go along. Working in the darker areas first seems to speed up the task and simplifies the matter of keeping the right color in the brush, for the color becomes weaker as we remoisten the brush from time to time. Doing the larger spots first also enables us to stop at any time we please, for often the spots that show on very close inspection are invisible at a normal viewing distance for the print. In such cases there is no reason for continuing the spotting of the places that cannot be seen.

This technique is adequate for any rough paper, and the spotting will dry down to a matte finish that matches the paper. However, if the paper has a luster, this dull finish in the spotting will show and we must add something to the liquid that will give it the same shine. A little mucilage or gum arabic mixed with the spotting color will cause it to dry with a luster, and one can easily determine the amount necessary to match the finish on which he is working. Remember, however, that spotting can be rubbed off, and a print that has been spotted is comparatively delicate. If some of the spotting color falls on the wrong place in the picture (the brush should never be nearly wet enough to drip) it can be removed with a bit of cotton moistened with clean water.

Working with the spotting colors and brush is gener-

Fig. 33. Spotting brush is held almost perpendicular to p int.

Fig. 34. Blemishes are stippled with the brush and disappear.

ally considered the easiest way to accomplish the task, but many workers prefer to use a pencil especially on matte and rough papers. For rough surfaces a carbon pencil sharpened to a very fine point works well, as it leaves a rough finish like that of the paper, and black lead pencils may be used on matte papers. When the pencil is used and a heavier deposit made than is wanted, the surplus can be wiped away with a gentle brush of the finger. Another method works with glossy paper. A finely pointed wax pencil of the proper color is dipped in liquid wax and then touched to the spot. On drying, the spot has the same shine as the paper and, if a small enough amount of wax was used, the spotting will not show. In many cases where difficulty is encountered in getting enough tone to stick to the paper, the surface may be roughened slightly with an etching knife to gain a tooth that will hold the color.

Spotting is another of the photographic processes that requires time and practice, but its proper use is so important that no photographer can afford to neglect it. The actual elimination of faults is not all that can be done to prints after they have reached this stage. It is still within our power to alter tones almost as we please, to accent highlights, darken areas that are too high in tone, and carry out any other changes desired. However, care must be exercised in following such a plan so as to make sure we do not introduce a "phony" note. We must see to it that everything we do to the print is justified and natural in the print itself.

For accenting highlights, introducing the catchlight in an eye where none existed before, and for lightening small or large areas, we can resort to the reduction technique described in Chapter II and, with a dilute solution of Farmer's Reducer raise the tone of any local area where it seems advisable. We must be careful, however, to use a very weak solution and to stop its action by rinsing the print in running water before it goes too far, for if the reducer is allowed to bleach out all the silver in any area we shall have created for ourselves a very difficult

Fig. 35. Straight print from a negative, showing some undesirable detail.

task with the spotting brush. A highlight on a nose is easily obtained by repeated applications with a brush or cotton of thin lines of the reducer in the desired places. In the repetitions it is best to vary the width of the lines to avoid a hard edge in the bleached area.

Similar uses for Farmer's Reducer will suggest themselves in various prints; remember always to stop the action well ahead of time and to wash the print thoroughly after it is completed. There will be less danger of bleaching the wrong places if the print is well soaked in water, placed on a tilted glass or the bottom of a tray, and wiped off with a viscose sponge before each application. If any of the chemical is spilled on the print, the whole print should be washed off at once.

Such a procedure, while it helps the general effect greatly, does not have the latitude of control that is to be found in either chalking or the oil tone process. Chalking, because it's a dry process and takes less time, is the more popular of these two and is easier to do and to control. The only materials necessary are finely powdered pumice, absorbent cotton, art gum or a kneaded eraser, and various colors of powdered French chalk, charcoal, or other similar materials. The process involves the roughening of the surface of the print and the rubbing into that surface the right color of chalk to obtain the desired tone. The chalk may be removed from large or small areas with the eraser, and the whole process is always under control as the chalk is not fixed to the surface until you are satisfied with the print. There are two ways of accomplishing this. The first consists of rubbing gently and evenly the entire surface of the print with the powdered pumice with a clean piece of cotton. By knocking the powder off and inspecting the print in a slanting light, one can check the evenness of the roughening. Another small piece of cotton is used to rub in the color wherever it is required.

Figs. 35 and 36 show what can be done with the chalking process. The whole print was rubbed down with the powdered pumice and then the color was applied

Fig. 36. Modifications have been made by the chalking process. Compare with Fig. 35.

in an even, light coat everywhere. Additional color was rubbed into the shadows with a small piece of cotton on a stump, and some extra color was rubbed into the other portions that needed darkening. Portions that needed lightening were rubbed with the eraser. A very light brushing with a loose wad of cotton removed most of the surplus powder, and holding the print by one corner and flicking it with a finger nail from the back brought the print to its final appearance.

At this stage the abrasion will show badly, but the color may be set permanently by steaming the surface; either by holding the print evenly in the jet of steam from a tea kettle, or by passing it very rapidly through water. If the steam process is used great care must be taken to subject each portion of the surface to the same amount of steam. If the water setting is to be used, a tray longer than the diagonal of the print is filled with water. Opposite corners are grasped while holding the print face down, and giving the print a slight backward curl, it is passed through the water as fast as possible, making sure that the whole surface is evenly wet. It is then hung up by the corner that entered the water first. The print must be allowed to become thoroughly dry before any change is made in its position. If its angle is altered while there is still free water on the surface, a streaked appearance will result. There is no way to remove the powder after the print has been set and dried, but of course if it has been removed while wet you can start over again when the print is dry.

Fig. 36, entitled "Mystery House," received other treatment before chalking. In order to give it more solidity, the house was lightened by local reduction with Farmer's Reducer on the side receiving the light. In the chalking treatment, the lower corners were darkened, the sky was darkened slightly in the upper righthand corner, and brightened directly behind the figures in order to concentrate attention at that point. The roadway underwent some treatment with the chalk in order to simplify the confusion of light and shade.

Figs. 11 and 30 show what may be accomplished by the oil tone process, which is excellent for semi-matte or rough papers. It is more or less similar to chalking in that we first work over the surface to darken the entire print, then remove the darkening material from the places we wish to keep light. The oil tone is supplied by a black or neutral oil paint which is dabbed over the surface of the print (securely fastened to a flat board or glass) with a wad of long-fibered cotton, and then rubbed into a smooth film. This thin layer of oil is rubbed into the surface of the print by a circular motion followed by straight rubs in every direction until the coating is perfectly uniform. A final rub with clean cotton leaves only a very thin transparent film that slightly tones the whole picture. We can use a colored oil, or warm the tone slightly by the addition of a small amount of burnt sienna to the black before it is applied. If the tone originally is too warm, the addition of a small amount of blue will serve to make it colder. The whole print is considerably darker in tone, work is done on the areas we wish to lighten with a clean wad of cotton containing a slight amount of photo color medium. This material removes the paint but leaves a surface comparable to that of the rest of the picture when it dries. As in the case of chalking, we do not want too hard a line between the cleaned places and those that have been darkened. The tones are blended at these edges after cleaning a somewhat smaller area than we want bright by a very gentle circular motion of a clean cotton wad. This means that there is still a scarcely noticeable tone in the clean areas, and these highlights are accented with color medium on a small wad of cotton or with the cotton on a stump. At the same time, we may wish to darken other areas even more than the general application has made them. To do this we apply more of the dark paint with the cotton or the stump, rubbing it into the paper thoroughly and blending it with the other tones so that it will not show as a smudge.

One final step in the finishing of the print will often

result in material improvement of its appearance. This is the application of wax or varnish, both of which protect the print and give it a high luster. Varnishing is usually preferred, because it is permanent and not affected by changes in humidity and temperature, while the wax may lose some of its luster in damp weather.

A number of varieties of wax for the purpose are available, and in applying them the print should be anchored securely with Scotch tape to a board so that the very small quantity of wax can be rubbed into the surface thoroughly and then polished vigorously without danger of wrinkling or cracking the emulsion. Use as little wax as possible, and after the coat is applied allow the print to remain until the wax is entirely dry; then repolish it well before mounting.

The varnish used should be the variety sold for photographic purposes. It should be applied freely with a soft camel hair brush—the 2″ size works quickly and well. Flow the varnish onto the print surface, using the brush as little as possible, then allow the varnish to dry completely before removing the print from the board. If it developes a tendency to curl, the back of the print can be given the same treatment; but this should never be done unless the paper is perfectly dry, or the water contained in it may cause bubbles in trying to escape.

So we find that much can be done to a picture even after it emerges from the wash and drys. Indeed, it is very often these after-treatments that make the difference between a print that is "pretty good," and one that receives universal acclaim.

# CHAPTER V

## HAND COLORING

H AND-COLORED photographs are decidedly un- pleasant to many people, but this feeling is probably caused by the fact that so few colored pictures are done properly. The average amateur suddenly realizes that he is working with colors and goes slightly haywire. Cheeks that should be pink turn out a brilliant crimson; lips that should look something like normal (if it is possible to define a normal color for lipstick these days) are col- ored with the brightest scarlet that can be had. Blonde hair turns into a horrible hemp yellow. No wonder we don't like colored photographs, and no wonder salons and competitions almost universally refuse to accept them!

However, everyone will admit that he has on rare occasions seen an attractive colored photograph—one well done. The difference between the kind of colored photograph we usually see and a good one is comparatively small. It lies principally in the quantity of coloring mate- rial used and the tones selected, rather than any inherent fault in the idea of hand-colored pictures. One that is well done depends for its strength on its natural realism, and subdues each color to the effect of the whole picture. The good picture blends each color into its neighbor as it occurs by reflection in nature, but unfortunately too many amateur color artists do not realize this and have not been willing to learn enough about color to justify their using it. A well-colored picture, and some under- standing of the simplicity of the process and its few fundamental principles, will usually convert the most stub- born opponent of color. If one tries his hand at coloring intelligently, he soon realizes the possibilities of this new medium, and will enjoy the extra realism and the change from pictures in monochrome.

The coloring kits available today are excellent and inexpensive. There are water colors and transparent oils, and the choice will depend entirely upon the preference of the user. The feeling seems to be quite general that the oils are rather easier to handle and more effective, but proponents of water colors obtain splendid results.

Let's first consider the general idea. The color will be a transparent layer deposited on a photograph whose details show through it. The result is that the various tones of one color are provided by the photographic image beneath it, and one has only to worry about selecting the proper shade to use. The color is applied in an even layer, using in one application as little as needed to cover the necessary area. Various colors are blended together to obtain the exact shade desired, and several layers are applied if necessary to deepen the tone or brighten the color. Adjacent tones are blended to make them look as they should.

Water colors can be used on any paper surface, and we need only follow the directions that come with the kit. The thing we must avoid is the use of too much color and lines that are too brilliant. Transparent oil colors differ in several ways. In the first place they work much better on a matte paper since they need to be rubbed into the surface more than do the water colors, which are absorbed. The oil pigments take a little longer to dry but can be controlled better by the beginner at coloring.

For either medium the print should be on white paper and slightly lighter than a black-and-white print would be. Sepia toning often helps portraits to show a good skin tone, but if the print is toned we must be careful that there are no deep shadows or chalky highlights. Its scale should be long and it should appear a little flat since we can build up the depth of the shadows successfully but cannot lighten them. The exact kind of print preferred will depend very much on our experience as we proceed with the coloring, and we shall soon find the type that gives best results. The materials needed are a drawing board or some other flat surface to which we can attach the print with Scotch tape or tacks, a color set, good quality, long-fibre cotton, a piece of glass for a pallet, and match sticks, heavy tooth picks or stumps with which to apply the color to small areas. We shall use swabs of the cotton in the larger sections.

For the beginner any of the regular oil kits sold on the market are splendid, and after he has gained some experience and some knowledge of what colors he needs the original purchase can be supplemented with other special colors. If he prefers to buy small tubes of the regular transparent oil colors he might begin with carmine, cheek, flesh, ultramarine, tree-green, cadmium yellow, burnt sienna, and brown. These paints are inexpensive and will color a great many prints. In addition to them one will need a tube of medium, a small bottle of turpentine, and a small tube of zinc white.

The print is attached to its support and placed in the same kind of light in which it will be hung. In black-and-white work this is less important, but colors applied in daylight seem flat in artificial light; and if the work is done by artificial light and the print shown in sunlight, the colors will seem much too strong and unnatural. We can, of course, use blue daylight bulbs if the print is to be shown in strong daylight, but it is much better to work in the same kind of light in which others will see the picture later. The next step is to squeeze on the pallet a small lump of each color that will be used. Then a small amount of the medium is squeezed directly onto the surface of the print, and rubbed thoroughly with a circular motion over the entire print area. Looking at it in an oblique light will show dull spots wherever the medium is lacking, and we must continue to rub until the whole surface is shining uniformly. Then with a clean dry cotton we remove as much medium as possible.

Now come the colors. Let us suppose we are coloring a portrait. Start at the face, then do the clothes, and finally finish the background. The first tone used is for the cheeks, but we must not standardize on some one color for this purpose. Five-year old Sally's complexion does not match that of Uncle Jim, the Arizona rancher and we must show the difference convincingly. The paint marked "flesh" is a good color for the average complexion but we must mix a little common sense and some other color with the "flesh" for variations in the age and complexion of our subject. We may add some of the "cheek" for the brighter face and the brown or burnt sienna for Uncle Jim. This is best done by taking a little of the "flesh" on a clean pad of cotton and rubbing it out on the pallet. Then, with the same cotton we pick up a tiny speck of the "cheek" and rub it into the "flesh" until they are thoroughly mixed. When the entire surface of the cotton shows an even tone we apply it to the face with a gentle circular motion over the entire skin area. We need not avoid the eyes, teeth, or any section that will finally have another color. A convenient thing about the oil colors is the ease with which they may be removed from any area. Now the print is checked carefully to see if the color is right, and any surplus color is removed with clean cotton. If the base color is not right (not the cheeks or lips, but the color of the skin itself) we can add the proper tone to the mixture made on the pallet and rub it over the same areas as we did before. This will blend with the color already applied, and we shall soon get it exactly right. The next step is the cheek color. Here again we must consider the general complexion and be sure to use almost none on Uncle Jim; little Sally would naturally show more color. The edges of the cheek color must blend well into the adjacent tones to avoid the painted spot effect. It should be impossible to determine where the cheek color begins and ends.

At this point the shadows appear rather dirty and gray, especially if the print was black-and-white rather than sepia. They may be relieved with a little "cheek" rubbed into the dark area with a small piece of cotton twisted on the end of a stick. The lips come next. They should be colored with the lip color, which is rubbed in with the stick and cotton without trying to do the whole job in one operation. Apply a little in each coat and continue until the effect is right. The upper lip, incidentally, will probably need more color than the lower. Be sure to blend colors where they meet, even though this blending may be very slight. An exception would, of course, occur where the red of the lip is outlined against white teeth.

And now comes one of the points in which we can do much to attain greater realism in the picture. Highlights on a moistened lip or on the nose and catchlights in the eyes have practically no color in nature; be sure to clean out these highlights carefully before the picture is finished. This is done with a tiny twist of cotton on a sharp stick; it is dipped into the medium and then very nearly dried on scrap paper. Most of the color will be taken up by this cotton, and that remaining will be loosened by the medium so that it can easily be removed with clean cotton. If more brilliance in the catchlights is desired, add the tinest speck of zinc white to them without rubbing it or blending it with the surrounding tones. The other highlights may be emphasized in the same way with the white, but with a very gentle circular motion to blend it into the surrounding color. The only real white in the picture will be the catchlights in the eyes. All other highlights will take on the faintest trace of their surrounding tone and be slightly soft and pearly.

The hair should be done next. In many cases a general all-over color is satisfactory, but occasionally this treatment gives a flat and muddy appearance. If so, snap up the effect by rubbing a darker tone of the same color into the shadows in the hair, and either removing some of the color from the lighter areas or adding a lighter tone to them. A thin dose of cadmium yellow and verona brown in about equal parts makes blonde hair, and burnt sienna with a trace of red or yellow gives good brown hair. If the subject's hair is black, gray, or white, the lightest possible application of blue will emphasize the color; white hair will sometimes benefit from judicious application of the zinc white in the highlights. Beware, though, of using too much white as it is very easy to let it get out of control and to give the picture a peculiar look.

The eyes need to be cleaned thoroughly of all flesh color with medium and then clean cotton on a stick. If the tone values in the eyes are right in the print, the color may be applied, but remember that the color is only in the iris; the pupil is always black. However, the tone of the iris is often too dark, especially in portraits made in incandescent light. In this case mix a tiny speck of the white with the eye color and apply it with cotton on the stick. Don't forget that the white is not transparent and that therefore the veins and radiating lines in the iris will not show plainly if too much color is used. We cannot be too careful in coloring the eyes, for they are always the most important part of a portrait and the attention is immediately centered on them.

While the clothing needs to be colored carefully it should not be made too prominent a part of the picture unless, of course, the cloth is the picture and the face is secondary to it as might be the case in fashion pictures. In the case of a pastel-colored dress there will be difficulty in applying a sufficiently small amount of color in a perfectly even tone, but the addition of a small amount of the white to the base color will fix this. Rub it over the whole dress area, and then with a small amount of white build up the shadows and finally clean out the highlights with clean cotton. It is here that the importance of making the print on white paper shows itself, for a tinted paper throws off the balance of these large highlights completely. Arms and hands, of course, receive the same treatment as the face, but here again clean highlights avoid the artificial look.

The background is important only as a setting for the portrait, and it must be kept subordinate to the rest of the picture even though it must harmonize with the more important areas. If the background is simple and unobtrusive, some cool color (on the blue side) will tend to push it farther behind the subject, while warm colors containing more yellow bring it forward considerably. If, however, the background is confusing and contains many light areas that distract one's attention from the picture, either darken them carefully and then color the whole background or use the opaque paint (such as the artists use) and simply paint over the background area. This requires considerable practice and is not particularly photographic, but it is often the easiest solution to the problem. A final inspection will show the success of our work. If we don't like it we can always remove all the paint with a swab of cotton soaked in turpentine, and begin over again.

The same fundamentals of color apply to the use of water colors, and the steps should be carried out in the same order. However, there are several differences in the handling of the two materials. Water colors may be used on any paper surface including glossy, while oils are best on rough surfaces, and either may be removed or lightened at will. With oils the desired tone is mixed on the palette and then applied. Water colors are put on in several applications that use little color each time and build up to the tone that looks best. This is the chief difference between the two media.

Water colors may be obtained in many forms. There are color cards, pots, tubes, or pieces of paper that are placed in water to color it. One set consists of dyed cotton that contains its own color and is moistened before the coloring is begun. Most of the water colors are best applied with a brush, though the blending may be done with clean cotton to prevent leaving too hard a line between adjacent colors.

In most cases there will be no difficulty in making the emulsion take the color. Sometimes glossy prints, especially if they have been ferrotyped, repel the color until the surface has been prepared by rubbing it gently with powdered chalk, or by a slight dampening with a 2% solution of ammonia, or with saliva. The chalk roughens the surface and causes the glossy finish to disappear, and the ammonia has a tendency to soften the emulsion and swell it, so the saliva is the preferred method.

If too much color is applied to any portion of the print, it may be removed with cotton dampened in a 2% solution of ammonia, or with the solution usually included in the commercial coloring kits that may be obtained nearly anywhere. Care must be taken to avoid too much soaking of the emulsion. When it is really wet, especially with an alkaline solution, the emulsion becomes very tender, so surplus liquid should be blotted off and the overwet spot allowed to dry before further application of the color.

The coloring of a landscape is handled in a fashion similar to portraits. Select colors that will fit the subject matter, and avoid the use of too much color in any part of the picture. Begin with the important elements in the scene and progress from there to the foreground, and finally the background and the sky. Remember to make the color scheme fit the apparent season, with warmer colors for summer and fall, slightly less yellow in the spring, and a decidedly bluish cast to winter pictures. Remember, too, that distant objects in nature are separated from us by an atmospheric haze that has a definitely bluish tint, and that we gain the effect of distance by mixing a trace of blue with the color of any object that must seem very far away.

Warmer tones, on the other hand, apparently bring objects closer to us, so grass in the foreground is slightly yellower than the same grass in the middle ground or background of the picture. Bushes and trees, too, respond to the same treatment. Landscapes will be much more effective and much more three-dimensional if we keep this fundamental fact in mind. Again we must be careful of our highlights. They will have at most only a slight choice of their own color, and in many cases they take on the color of nearby objects by reflection. A girl's white dress for example is definitely greenish at the bottom if she is standing on the grass and her white hat will have a greenish cast if she is under a tree. Water reflects the color of the sky, and the difference between the two colors is simply one of tone, the reflected color being a little darker than the original.

Seascapes require a greener blue than do snow scenes or landscape skies, and the proper emphasis of highlights on white foam is vital. Here again one must avoid the use of too much white, and each bit of white will either be that of the print itself or made with a slight mixture of white to the basic color.

There is always the strong temptation to use the coloring process to put clouds in an otherwise bald print, and it can be done very pleasingly provided we do not attempt to show the clouds in too great detail. Nor should we attempt to make them too white. In most cases the best procedure will be to tone the whole sky the kind of blue we prefer and then build the clouds by removing the color but without adding any white.

Work thoughtfully; keep colors in harmony and subdued in tone; blend adjacent colors; remember that highlights are nearly always white. Follow these rules and your hand-colored pictures will have a natural realism that everyone will enjoy.

## CHAPTER VI

## MOUNTING

E VEN after the print is finished it is not ready to be shown to best advantage. Just as a new house looks bare and lonely until its setting of shrubbery and grass is in place, so does our pictures need to be framed and set off in a manner that will add to its effectiveness and make an attractive finished unit. We might describe the mount of a picture as the window through which we see that part of the scene which the artist has selected, while the edges of the window cut off the remaining and less valuable sections of the landscape.

The value and the contribution that a proper frame adds to a picture is easily proved by looking first at the print alone and comparing the effect it gives with that of an identical print mounted and ready for hanging. The mount, by its very power to add to the value of the print, may also detract, and there are many elements to be considered. In selecting the mount that will do most for a print we must decide upon the size, color, and texture of the mounting material, the location of the print in the mount area, and the use to which the picture is to be put.

The purpose of the print may also be a determining factor in the size and material of the mount. Salons have standardized their size and color, requirements; almost all of them demand, or at least prefer, a 16"x20" mount of light color which may be hung vertically regardless of whether the picture is horizontal or vertical. This is because most salons are exhibited under glass in permanent frames or racks that require this vertical dimension. They have established this rule not only for convenience in hanging but also to assist the committee in presenting the show in an attractive manner. There is undoubtedly some thought that this rough standardization places the interest in the picture where it belongs rather that in some of the elaborate and complicated mountings that would otherwise be devised.

The first fundamental of effective mounting is simplicity. The mount frames the picture and is supporting and helpful detail of its presentation. It would to a large degree defeat its main purpose if anything about it caught the eye of the observer and drew his attention from the important thing—the picture itself. However, some amount of ornament, such as a border (though it has a utilitarian function rather than a purely decorative purpose) is not only permissible but often helpful. Titles and signatures must not be allowed to be become so ornate that the mind of the observer is more intrigued by them than by the picture they are supposed to describe. This does not mean that we must become stereotyped in our mounting methods. Just as varying treatments of different subjects require their own surfaces and tones, so the mount must agree with the picture and blend harmoniously with its thought and mood of expression.

With the picture in hand, then, we must first decide on the use to which it will be put and on the type of mounting that will be best for that purpose. For example, if we plant to carry the picture with many others for long distances as is the lot of many lecturers, the weight of the mount becomes important, and flat mounting on a single card is indicated. On the other hand, if the print is to be subjected to careless handling we might prefer to use the heavier cut-out mount made of two cards. Again, if the surface of the print is delicate, we may wish to cover it permanently with cellophane, or supply a protective paper flap to cover it when it is not on display. If the picture's main purpose is the entertainment of our friends who will hold it in their hands, a light card or bristol board mount may be adequate, and if the prints are small we may prefer to put them in some type of scrap book or album.

With the general type of mounting decided upon, we

can then think about the material and its color and texture
This, of course, depends largely on the surface of the
print, its size, its tone, and to some degree, its subject
matter.   A subject for which glossy paper is appropriate
and which is printed on that material will often be better
on a smooth mount, but the same mount is not appropriate for a picture printed on a very rough surface
Here rougher mount is indicated.   The important factor
in making the decision is the effect of the whole as we
look at it.

Even more significant is the color of the mount and
its suitability to that of the print.   A print on white
paper should never be mouned on cream or buff cardboard
unless it has been toned to some shade of brown that
fits in with that color.   Blue toned prints demand a white
mount, and as a general rule the white mount is always
acceptable.   Any other tone should be used only when
the print definitely demands it.

The remaining chief consideration is the location of
the print in the mount area.   As a general rule, the
width of the mount around the picture will be the same
at the top and sides and greater at the bottom, as shown
in Fig. 37A.   In the case of an 11x14 print placed hori-
zontally on a 16x20 mount as in Fig. 37B, we may prefer
to make the top distance greater than the two sides which
are, of course, equal.   It may be, however, that a small
picture that must for some reason be shown in a comparatively large mount will look better if it is placed
differently as in Figs. 37C and 37D, where the boat running diagonally downward is given space to move in
the mount, and the boy looking up also a long distance in
front of him.

Figure 38 illustrates another exception to the usual
spacing rule in that the top margin is less than that at the
sides.   The picture is a bas relief made by superimposing
a positive and negative of the same picture but slightly
out of register and printing through the composite.   Its
shape was determined by the composition and not by
the dimensions of the paper available, and to give a space

A

B

C

D

Fig. 37. Suggestion for placing the print, picture title, and photographer's signature in the mount area. Print location depends on size and picture composition, as explained in text.

Fig. 38. This print requires wider margins on sides than on top.

at the top equal to that of the sides would place the print too low on the mount. Other unusual cases will often demand some departure from normal standards, and we should never fear to be different provided there is a good explanation in the picture for our variation.

The simplest mounting of all is actually no mount, as shown in Fig. 39, but simply an ink or pencil line drawn around the print equidistant from top and sides and generally a little farther from the bottom edge of the picture area. This necessitates the use of fairly large paper for the size of the print, but it is a very effective mounting for pictures which are to be handed to friends for their inspection or placed in albums. The location of the picture on the sheet will, of course, follow the general rules for the placement of a print in a mount.

A somewhat similar effect is obtained by the so-called plate-sunk mounting that also requires the print on oversize paper. The print is laid face down on a sheet of paper about its own thickness, but cut to the dimensions of the space inside the desired plate sinking. By transmitted light we determine the proper location of this sheet in relation to the print itself and, still working by transmitted light, we run the end of a knitting needle or a tooth brush handle around the edge of the sheet, forming a depression in the print paper. The pressure must be even, and it is better to have the print slightly damp to avoid cracking the emulsion. In many cases a print thus plate-sunk may be mounted in a cutout mount to good effect, and if this is done the space between the plate-sunk line and the edge of the cutout will follow the general rules of spacing. There is almost no limit to the methods we may adopt in framing our prints, but we must always avoid distracting influences. The mount frames and isolates the print from its surroundings, and it would be silly to have it cause the very trouble it ostensibly seeks to avoid.

Let's look at some of the methods by which prints can be mounted. The first is the single flat mounting in which the print is trimmed to frame the picture exactly and then

Autumn —

Irene Draper

Fig. 39. A border line on the print provides an effective finish.

fastened onto the face of the card. Glue and ordinary paste are most unsatisfactory as they cause the mount to bend and may have a bad effect on the print itself. In fact, any cementing material that contains water is likely to be dangerous, and therefore rubber cement or dry mounting tissue are preferred.

In either case, take the trimmed print, measure its width and subtract this distance from the width of the mount. Divide the distance by two and draw faint lines on the mount at this resulting dimension from its edge at both sides and top. The height of the print, of course, determines the location of the fourth line. If the print is to be mounted with rubber cement, paint the face of the mount and the back of the print with the material and allow them to dry. It will not matter if the surface of the print outside the picture area receives the cement as it is easily rubbed off afterward without damaging the mount. Here some care must be taken since the two coated surfaces stick together firmly and permanently as soon as they touch. If we wish to take a chance, we can align one edge of the print with the proper pencil mark and rub the print to the mount with a rolling motion from that edge. A safer technique is the one illustrated in Figs. 40 and 41. A piece of waxed paper is laid over the mount so that it covers the entire cemented area with the exception of perhaps $\frac{1}{8}$ inch along the length of one pencil mark. The print is then laid on the wax paper and lined up with all four marks. When it is located exactly, slight pressure along the edge that is not protected by the wax paper holds it firmly in place. Lift the opposite side of the print and remove the wax paper. Then, beginning at the edge which has been attached, press the print to the mount.

If the print surface is delicate, it is better to cover it with a piece of paper as shown in Fig. 41 before pressing it down, and such protection is always advisable before it is rubbed flat to assure perfect contact everywhere. A print so mounted is permanent, but it may be removed by leaving it in the sun for several hours after which it can be peeled off. A temporary mounting, of course,

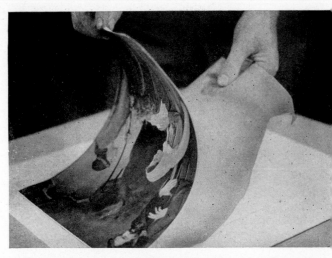

Fig. 40. Wax paper on cemented mount aids in placing the print.

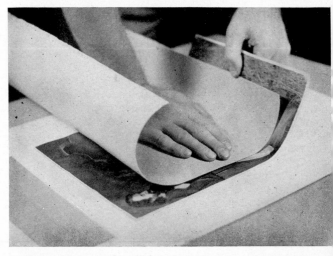

Fig. 41. Protect print surface with paper when applying pressure.

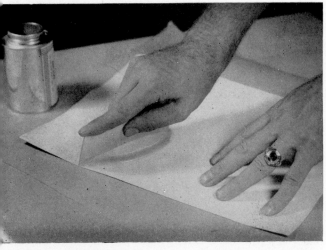

Fig. 42. Method of applying rubber cement to back of the print.

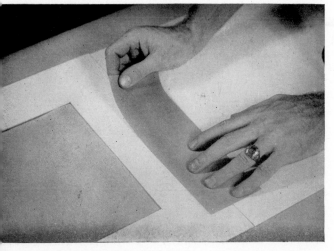

Fig. 43. Showing method of hinging cutout mask to print mount.

requires rubber cement on only one surface and the application of the print to the mount while the cement is still wet. In either case the cement should be applied as evenly as possible. Fig. 42 shows an easy way of accomplishing this by pouring a quantity of the cement on the print and spreading it evenly with a piece of cardboard. Dry mounting tissue is a transparent sheet material that is inserted between the print and the mount over the entire surface and then made to stick to both by the application of heat. This material is on the market under several names, and small electric irons can be procured to heat it and press the surfaces together.

Another method of mounting is the single card cutout in which an opening of the required size and shape is cut in the mount and the print fastened to the back with Scotch tape or some other adhesive material. In appearance this is very similar to the double cutout, but it offers much less protection to the print, and the corners of the mount are more likely to be damaged in shipment or handling. It is, however, lighter to carry than the double mount and of course costs less since only one mounting card is required.

Fig. 43 shows the construction of a hinged double mount. Two cards are required, one of which is cut out exactly as was the mount for the single cutout method. This card is then laid face down on a table with its end touching another similar but uncut card which is face up. With the two held firmly together, a strip of adhesive paper tape is laid over the joint between the two as shown, and they are then folded together, the tape serving as a hinge. The print is placed between the two cards and moved about until it is properly centered in the opening. A weight on the print will hold it in place until the top flap is opened and guide lines are drawn around the edges on the bottom card. Mounting is best done with rubber cement across the top edge of the print. A strip of Scotch tape across the top edge serves as a temporary mount, so that one can substitute some other print whenever desired. If the finished mount is to be as substantial as possible, use cement

Fig. 44. A narrow black border around the print is often effective.

or glue to fasten the two parts of the mount together. Make sure that the glue extends to the edges of the mount, but do not use any within a half inch of the print. When the glue is dried under pressure we have a strong permanent mounting that is most satisfactory.

There is good reason for supporting the print only at the top and not gluing the mounts together right up to the edge of the print. Photographic paper swells and contracts with changes in the atmosphere, and if the print is fastened all over or around the edges, there is danger of future wrinkles and bubbles, but with the support at the top only and freedom of the other edges to move between the mounts the print will remain perfectly flat.

Now we are ready for the signature. title, and anything else that must be done on the front of the mount. As a general rule, the title is at the lower left corner of the print and the maker's signature at the lower right. They should be written or printed plainly so that they may be read at a glance, and this done so simply that there is no thought in the mind of the observer of anything except the message they convey. An ornate or elaborate signature or title is definitely bad and should be avoided. It may be desirable to add some simple decorative line like that shown in Fig. 39. Such a border often gives a feeling of added depth to the window effect of the mount. The size and complexity of this additional trimming is entirely a matter of taste, but the simpler it is kept the more effective it will be.

As a variation of the flat single mount we may wish to enclose the print in a dark border before it reaches the mount. In the case of Fig. 44, the dark line was made in the print, but a similar effect can be achieved by first fastening to the mount a piece of black paper a little larger each way than the dimensions of the print. We see an occasional picture in which two such papers have been used for a two-tone border, and sometimes it is very effective. However, a single border is safer as it avoids the danger of making the whole mounting seem too complicated and fussy. We may, however, find that such a plan with perhaps an off-center mounting of both print and papers adds materially to the effectiveness of a Christmas card picture, and a touch of color thus introduced may be a good idea.

If one wishes to give a print an additional protection regardless of the method employed in mounting it, he can add a protective flap of paper by cutting it the width of the mount but somewhat longer than the greatest dimension of the mounting card. The extra length is folded over to the back of the mount and there cemented in place with the cement extending to the top of the card. The paper then may be folded back to disappear behind the mount when the picture is being shown. An alternate method that is widely used to protect a delicate surface or a color print utilizes cellophane or thin Kodaloid as a permanent transparent covering. It is stretched tightly over the face of the mount and held on the back with Scotch tape.

Whatever method of mounting is preferred, remember the guiding principle and make sure that the mount is a contributing but definitely subordinate factor in the presentation of the picture. In simplicity will be found its true effectiveness.

# CHAPTER VII

## THE TITLE

IN the last chapter we passed over the question of titles with only a word about the need for keeping them simple. However, the proper title shown in a way that fits the picture can do much to set the mood of the print and to make those who see it look at it from more nearly the viewpoint of the photographer. A picture tells the story as much by the association of ideas and the train of thought that it sets into motion as by the subject matter it actually contains. It is for us as photographers to include an unmistakable story in the picture itself. But since so much of that story begins outside the picture we can help it to express the one we have chosen with a title that starts the proper thinking in the mind of the observer. To label the picture of a cow "Bossy" means little, but to call it "Portrait of a Lady" immediately sets up a stronger reaction, and the print is likely to be remembered as much for the idea as for its excellence as a photograph.

Too often the photographer makes a picture for lack of anything better to do. He is not definitely inspired by the scene, and the print arouses little enthusiasm. But he feels that the print needs a title, and after deep study of the question for several seconds he comes up with something like "Spring" or "Rhythm" or some other abstract title that might fit any of a number of pictures and yet not supply any great assistance to any one of them. If a title is to mean something, it must be suggested by something in the picture or by the line of thinking that the picture sets into motion. If the picture has no underlying idea and is just another photograph, a title can probably do very little for it, and the picture itself is not likely to suggest one.

However, the shot of a deserted house may express very different emotions when we give it various titles like "Mystery House," "Yesterday's Glory," or "Deserted." The picture is the same in all three cases, but the difference in the titles supplies a springboard for our thought, and we find that each of these titles makes the picture tell an entirely different story. By the same token, a title that does not fit the picture or whose connection with it is far-fetched is likely to result in confusion and, therefore, in a lessened appreciation of the whole. It behooves us, then, to choose our titles carefully. It will probably be easier if we make a mental note of the emotion we feel when we see the subject matter of the picture. This emotion or the title that suggested itself is likely to be the one that will be most valuable in adding to the strength of the picture. Later thoughts may be improvements, but too often they tend to become artificial and therefore weak.

So much for the idea of the title and what it can do for us. Mechanically too, the title must fit. A high-key picture of a glamourous girl called "Summer Beauty" would not be lettered in the same way that we would write the sarcastic title in the same words under a picture of a burly, sunburned truck driver; nor would it be appropriate to use the same system of marking for a stiff architectural scene and an attractive and humorous picture of a small baby. Yet how often do we find the photographer spending hours on the print and mount, and then ignoring the final touch by scrawling almost anything underneath it. Just as the title is a part of the picture from the emotional standpoint, it should be an integral part mechanically. We should choose the method of lettering as carefully as we do the words.

For the architectural scene block letters or Roman capitals are fitting, and will carry out the idea of the picture. Such lettering, however, will not be as effective for the title "Speed" beneath a flying bird. There we would want a more delicate and less formal design—something more expressive of the lightness and dash of the bird in flight.

Titles in a foreign language are usually less valuable to the picture than they would be in English—we say "usually" because there are some pictures that do create a better reaction with a foreign title. The picture is the controlling factor, and if our mind is truly satisfied only with one particular title regardless of the language used, then that title is the one that fits the picture and the only one that we should put beneath it.

Signatures, too, should be simple. The elaborate signature, full of flourishes or worked into a complicated design, is likely to attract more attention than the picture. Its only purpose is to tell the world the name of the maker, and when it has accomplished this, it can do nothing more. Many workers prefer to sign the picture in the same kind of lettering that they use for the title, while others use their regular written signature for all pictures. The uniformity of design in the lettering has a great many arguments in its favor from the standpoint of unity and balance, but how we shall sign ours is a matter of taste and opinion. If it pleases us and introduces no jarring note it is the method we should adopt. The lettering itself, whether it be for a title or signature, should be bold enough to be read easily and at a glance.

A penciled handwriting is probably found most often, but the pencil should not be too soft and the color of the lettering—no matter what the medium—should be slightly lighter than the darker areas of the print. Black India ink is blacker than the deepest darks in a print and, therefore, lettering with this ink is generally more prominent than the picture unless the lines are extremely fine. If one prefers to use ink it will probably be better to get white or gray ink and adjust its color to suit the individual print. A dark gray ink will be suitable for almost any print, but sticklers for uniformity often use ink or pencil a few shades lighter in tone but the same color as the print.

Incidentally, when a rough mount is used we may have difficulty in making the lettering smooth. This can be overcome to a large degree by rubbing the area in which we wish to write with a tooth brush handle or some other smooth object that will not mark the mount. If the stylus is drawn back and forth along a straight edge no one will be able to see its marks without very close inspection. The same trick often helps us to draw lines around the print by supplying a smooth path in which the pencil or pen follows. The lines are nothing in themselves except a sort of fence which prevents our attention from jumping out of the picture. If they are too heavy we will pay more attention to the fence than to the picture, and their purpose will be defeated.

We have seen in Fig. 44 how a dark enclosing line may be introduced in making the print. Fig. 45 shows how we can introduce the title in the print too. In many cases a properly arranged title in the print area can be used to balance an otherwise off-center picture. A three-quarter length portrait, for example, may have a large empty space above and in front of the head. The name of the subject or the title of the print can be worked into this space to form not only an attractive title, but also a valuable compositional element. In Fig. 45 the title was etched directly on the print, a method which is satisfactory if only one print is to be made. However, if the final print is to be the result of a diapositive and an enlarged negative, we can supply the title in light letters by lettering it on the final negative or in black letters on the print by working on the diapositive.

It is unwise to attempt to letter a title on a small negative that is subsequently to be enlarged, because any imperfections in the lettering will be magnified. If gray letters will be satisfactory and the print offers an area that is suitable, we can do the lettering with a mixture of India ink and water glass (sodium silicate) on a piece of unscratched celluloid that is big enough to cover the entire print, and place this sheet over the printing paper during part of the exposure. The shorter the time we leave the sheet in place, the lighter the tone of the letters will be, and if we make the whole exposure through this sheet, the letters will be white. This will probably not be entirely satisfactory, since the thickness of the celluloid separates the lettering and the paper, and the edges of the letters will not be clear and sharp. However, we can work by transmitted light and trace the letters in reverse on the back of the celluloid, so that they are directly in contact with the emulsion during the exposure, and then the lettering will be crisp and distinct.

The type of lettering used will depend upon the subject matter and the treatment we have given it, and the same ideas will apply to this method of titling as to the printing of the title on the mount. Another method for obaining white lettering on the face of the print involves the use of an iodine bleach which can be applied with a ruling or lettering pen without fear of its spreading. Black letters can be drawn with India ink on the print, but this is not as pleasing since the letters become too prominent, the ink has a different shine from the rest of the surface, and is darker in tone than any other area. The result is a title that is likely to become the most prominent thing in the picture. Almost always such titles should have very thin lines and be delicate in their drawing. However, a rough, tough, and ugly character would require a bolder treatment, and heavier lines could be used.

If we feel that our lettering ability is too weak for this kind of work, we can have the printer set up the necessary type and give us one good proof on a glossy surface paper or find the necessary printed matter elsewhere, and copy the lettering on Process film. This film has a high-contrast emulsion that is used almost entirely for black-and-white line work, and with it (with short exposures and long development in a contrasty developer) we can reproduce the lettering in the size we need with a negative that is absolutely opaque in the paper area and clear film in the letters. If the negative is less contrasty, a short immersion

ST·PAUL'S     1765

Fig. 45. The picture title can be included on the print itself.

in Farmer's Reducer will clear up the letters. One method of using such a negative is to determine the exact position for the letters and print them with the light of the enlarger. The negative is placed on the sensitive paper and all the remaining surface masked off. After an initial exposure the negative and mask are removed and the print exposed as usual.

An occasional picture is sufficiently valuable to warrant its being framed. The simplest framing and one which is very effective involves the fastening of the mount either between two glasses or to one glass with black gummed tape that will form a border around the edges. Another very satisfactory display arrangement for home use or for clubs is the Braquette, a metal gadget that holds the top and bottom of the mount either between glass or without it, and which may be attached to the wall with a hidden screw or hung from the picture moulding. The pictures may be changed quickly and easily, an event that may prove a real blessing to the family. We will find that hanging a picture on the wall and living with it for a time will be the best method of learning whether or not it is good. It may be hard on members of the photographer's family, but they have to become accustomed to such treatment.

If we remember that our picture is complete and finished only where there is nothing more that we can do to help it, we will find that it will get a better reception.

# CHAPTER VIII

## NOVELTIES

MOST pictures are made for the sheer fun of their making, but we can often use our photographic knowledge to good advantage in more practical ways. A good photograph may serve as the basis for an attractive and individual lamp shade, Christmas card, book plate, letter-head, or any other of a number of useful items. Christmas presents often can be made at small cost and presented to people for whom we could not hope to buy a suitable gift. The personal touch and unique quality of such a present guarantees its success. Let us consider some of these and the methods to follow in making them, with the thought that these suggestions will lead to other and more original products.

The Christmas card problem is difficult to solve; the cards we would prefer to send are often beyond our financial reach, and those we can afford are being sent by everybody. However, if we make the cards ourselves, we can turn out exactly what we wish with the certainty that those who receive them cannot receive the same thing from anyone else. The foundation of our Christmas card is, of course, a suitable picture. Styles have changed, and these days almost any subject can be used, though most people still prefer a picture that includes something of the Christmas season.

Masks, lettering negatives, and embossers are included in each of several kits that are available in the stores. One can make his own mask with little difficulty and produce a card that is totally unlike any other. A card like Fig. 46 involves nothing more than a good idea and

Fig. 46. Christmas cards which are intended for intimate friends of the family do not necessarily require any lettering.

some skill in the making of the original photograph. Cards of this type are often sent to intimate friends without lettering of any kind, however, any of the methods discussed before may be used to include a greeting or signature. A picture of the baby is universally pleasing, and the whole family or the home make good subjects. The card itself may be a straight photograph without legend or mount. If we wish to print the greeting or the signature as individual units separated from the picture on the card, we can do so by following the directions in the kit or design something different. A mask of opaque paper can be cut to frame the picture and hold the negative in the right place, while other openings carry the greeting, signature, or other decorative negatives. The final card may be a single sheet or a double fold that must be opened to read the message inside.

While it may be monotonous to print, develop, fix, wash, and dry seventy-five or a hundred prints from the

A tabletop picture and snapshot cutout were combined and copied to produce the unusual card idea shown above.

This type of greeting is not hard to make. A red card with printed legend was used as a mount for the picture.

FIG. 47

WINTER HAVEN (TABLE TOP)     E.E.D.

Fig. 48. A tabletop picture serves as the illustration for this attractive greeting. The mount is a folded piece of fancy paper.

same negative, the satisfaction of knowing that we have mailed a unique and personal card is well worth the time and trouble involved. Economy is a secondary motive, and our main object is the better card. If we produce only a poor copy of something else we might far better buy our cards. Nor should we forget that our skill as photographers will be established in the minds of the recipients of those cards by their excellence. We cannot afford to send out a card that has something wrong with it, so we must make them carefully and not hesitate to discard any that are less than perfect.

Place cards, post cards, birth announcements, and other similar mailing pieces are easily made, and have the same unique quality. Indeed, there is no limit to the number of things that the ingenuity of the photographer can produce. Take bookplates, for example. An attractive

Fig. 49. A simple method of introducing lettering into a picture was employed in making this bookplate; it is described below.

photograph is covered with a sheet of Traceoline on which the necessary lettering is drawn with a pencil. In the one shown in Fig. 49, the lettering was simply penciled on the Traceoline, and the name backed by a panel of white paper. The combination was then photographed to the desired size, and as many as were needed made by contact printing. The same technique can be used to produce more elaborate items with any desired degree of complexity in the design and lettering.

Bookmarks may be made simply by gluing two long, thin prints back to back in any shape that pleases us. A colored transparency can be placed between two pieces of celluloid to make a combination paper cutter and ornament. A method that works well involves three layers of celluloid, the outer two quite thick, and the center one about the thickness of a Kodachrome transparency. In the

handle of the "dagger," if that is the design chosen, we cut an oblong opening (in the thin piece of celluloid) the exact size of the transparency. One surface of this piece is painted with acetone and cemented to one of the thick pieces of celluloid. It is kept under pressure until it dries. The transparency is then inserted into its hole and the other celluloid layer is cemented in place as was the first one. If the work is done carefully, with a slight bend in the celluloid as the pieces are joined, there will be no bubbles and the celluloid dagger appears to be one solid piece. With a sharp knife we can smooth out the edges of the joint and whittle a sharp enough blade for a paper cutter. If the transparency used is an attractive picture and one that definitely connects us with it in the minds of the recipient, such a knife makes an excellent gift for the hard-to-please friend.

Lamp shades appear more difficult to make than they

Fig. 51. The print
is held in place by
a celluloid cover.

really are. The one shown in Fig. 50 was made by selecting a plain shade at the store and covering it with a trun-
cated cone of fireproof celluloid (Fig. 51). The ends of
the strip that forms this cone are cemented together with
acetone as suggested for the paper cutter. The celluloid
shade is raised and the photograph placed between the
celluloid and the original lamp shade. The print may be
left oblong, but it will be better if it is cut in the shape
of a wedge (Fig. 52). Several of them may be arranged
around the shade. Thin, singleweight paper or the double-
coated thin papers especially made for transparencies are
best, and the prints should be rather contrasty.

When using the double-coated papers we can color the
back of the prints, working by transmitted light, so that
the pictures appear in monochrome when the lamp is
turned off and in color when it is lighted. A more expensive, but intriguing lampshade may be made by substituting

101

Fig. 52. Print for use on lamp shade is cut as shown here.

large color transparencies for the prints, but these require a larger camera and run the cost up considerably.

Prints on Ivora or Opal plates have many uses for miniatures in lockets or small frames. Often a small print on such material and inexpensively framed is more acceptable as a gift than a large cabinet-size portrait. If we were to suggest all the gifts that can come from our camera this book would need many more pages between its covers. It is the intent of this chapter to supply inspiration and ideas rather than actual suggestions, and our ingenuity will direct us farther along the road.

Favors, cards, and gimcracks that we make photographically must be well done or they will find their rightful resting place in the waste basket. If we attempt to turn our hobby to practical things, let it be done in a manner and with a skill comparable to that of the professional workman. If we fall short of that high standard, we have indeed failed.

102

# CONCLUSION

The various procedures and methods discussed in this book have one common aim—the production of the finest and most perfectly presented photographs that we are able to turn out. Many of the processes are extremely simple in use, while others, though simple in theory, require long practice before they can be carried through with complete success. It is hoped that the suggestions in these pages will not only point out the causes for some failures and the remedies that might be applied, but will also inspire the amateur to set a standard of excellence that allows him to be satisfied with nothing less than the very best work he can do. Too many photographers make a print that is a good print, and accept it with the comment "it is good enough." For the serious photographer no print can be good enough unless he is convinced that he cannot improve it in any way.

A famous exhibitor once said "Learn the fundamentals and then make pictures, more pictures, and more pictures." We know the fundamentals or we would not be reading this book. His advice can only be improved upon by a slight addition—make more pictures, but try to utilize in every one the information gained from the last, and make each one a little better than the one before.